Dame Julie Andrews' Botched Vocal Cord Surgery

Katherine Meehan is a writer from North Carolina. She holds an MA in Creative Writing from the University of Oxford, and her work has appeared in journals on both sides of the Atlantic, including *The Canvas, The Moth, The Kenyon Review, Magma,* and *Crannog*. She lives in Reading with her family.

Dame Julie Andrews' Botched Vocal Cord Surgery

and Other Poems

Katherine Meehan

Also by Two Rivers Poets

David Attwooll, *The Sound Ladder* (2015)
Charles Baudelaire, *Paris Scenes* translated by Ian Brinton (2021)
William Bedford, *The Dancers of Colbek* (2020)
Kate Behrens, *Man with Bombe Alaska* (2016)
Kate Behrens, *Penumbra* (2019)
Kate Behrens, *Transitional Spaces* (2022)
Conor Carville, *English Martyrs* (2019)
David Cooke, *A Murmuration* (2015)
David Cooke, *Sicilian Elephants* (2021)
Tim Dooley, *Discoveries* (2022)
Jane Draycott, *Tideway* (re-issued 2022)
Jane Draycott & Lesley Saunders, *Christina the Astonishing* (re-issued 2022)
Claire Dyer, *Interference Effects* (2016)
Claire Dyer, *Yield* (2021)
John Froy, *Sandpaper & Seahorses* (2018)
James Harpur, *The Examined Life* (2021)
Maria Teresa Horta, *Point of Honour* translated by Lesley Saunders (2019)
Ian House, *Just a Moment* (2020)
Philippe Jaccottet, *In Winter Light* translated by Tim Dooley (2022)
Rosie Jackson & Graham Burchell, *Two Girls and a Beehive* (2020)
Rosie Jackson, *Love Leans over the Table* (2023)
Gill Learner, *Chill Factor* (2016)
Gill Learner, *Change* (2021)
Sue Leigh, *Chosen Hill* (2018)
Sue Leigh, *Her Orchards* (2021)
Becci Louise, *Octopus Medicine* (2017)
Mairi MacInnes, *Amazing Memories of Childhood, etc.* (2016)
Steven Matthews, *On Magnetism* (2017)
Steven Matthews, *Some Other Where* (2023)
Henri Michaux, *Storms under the Skin* translated by Jane Draycott (2017)
Kate Noakes, *Goldhawk Road* (2023)
René Noyau, *Earth on Fire and other Poems* translated by Gérard Noyau with Peter Pegnall (2021)
James Peake, *Reaction Time of Glass* (2019)
James Peake, *The Star in the Branches* (2022)
Peter Robinson & David Inshaw, *Bonjour Mr Inshaw* (2020)

Peter Robinson, *English Nettles* (re-issued 2022)
Peter Robinson, *Retrieved Attachments* (2023)
Lesley Saunders, *Nominy-Dominy* (2018)
Lesley Saunders, *This Thing of Blood & Love* (2022)
Jack Thacker, *Handling* (2018)
Robin Thomas, *The Weather on the Moon* (2022)
Susan Utting, *Half the Human Race* (2017)
Jean Watkins, *Precarious Lives* (2018)

First published in the UK in 2023 by Two Rivers Press
7 Denmark Road, Reading RG1 5PA.
www.tworiverspress.com

© Katherine Meehan 2023

The right of the poet to be identified as the author of this work
has been asserted by her in accordance with the Copyright, Designs
and Patents Act of 1988.

All rights reserved. No part of this publication may be reproduced,
stored in or introduced into a retrieval system, or transmitted,
in any form, or by any means (electronic, mechanical, photocopying,
recording or otherwise) without the prior written permission
of the publisher.

ISBN 978-1-915048-11-0

2 3 4 5 6 7 8 9

Two Rivers Press is represented in the UK by Inpress Ltd
and distributed by BookSource.

Cover illustration and design by Sally Castle
Text design by Nadja Robinson and typeset in Janson and Parisine

Printed and bound in Great Britain by CMP (UK), Poole

Acknowledgements

Poems in this collection have appeared previously at *Bath Magg*, *Interpreter's House*, *Neon*, *Crannog*, *Magma*, *Anthropocene*, *The Moth*, *Marathon Literary Review*, *The Fortnightly Review*, *Lunate*, *The Canvas*, and *Brittle Star*.

I would like to thank Peter Robinson for his support. Huge thanks also to Makomborero Kasipo, Logan Scott, Ioan Marc Jones, Annalise Torcson, and Gabriella Attems for their help along the way. And finally, many thanks to Luke Elson for hanging in there with me.

Contents

A Motivational Poster | 1
Dame Julie Andrews' Botched Vocal Cord Surgery | 2
Aubade | 3
Desiderata | 4
The Wedding at Cane Creek Farm | 5
Every Little Helps | 6
Carol | 7
Night, Lamp, Street, Pharmacy | 8
Princess Cottongrass | 9
Goat Willow | 10
Castle Meadows | 11
Follow the Gleam | 13
That Month We Walked | 14
Nymphette | 15
Pastoral Care | 16
Thinking About the Chicken Bridge Murder While Riding in a Truck | 17
God's Smoking Lounge | 19
Grendel Mama | 20
Bear Hunter's Ballad | 21
Hemdean Valley/Anthem | 22
Street Party | 23
The Gearagh | 24
The Twelve Swans | 27
The Elvers | 28
Elegy | 29
Lemure | 33
The Rail Replacement Bus at Surbiton | 34
The Museum of Bad Art | 35
A Compendium of Losers | 36
Run for Your Life! | 38
Nabokov's Genitalia Cabinet | 40
Mercury in Retrograde | 41
No One Comes from No One | 42
The Pioneers | 43

The Extrovert | 44
At the Café des Artistes, 2006 | 45
Tuesday in Bracknell | 46
Eating a Danish Alone on a Friday | 47
Cholsey Station: Staring Down the Well of the Present Moment | 48
Double Rainbow | 49
Sourwood | 50
Notes on the Eleusinian Mysteries | 52
Happy New Year! | 55
To Edward D Wood Jr – An Invocation | 56
The Opposite of Ocean | 57
Enta Geweorc | 58
The Pleasure Club | 59

A Motivational Poster

Better times are coming
for someone.
Things can get worse.
And they will and they won't.

If you are crying, ask your tears:
what is the point of water?
Laugh and if you can't
laugh, laugh

Dame Julie Andrews' Botched Vocal Cord Surgery

The surgeon's voice was chipper: *Julie Andrews, you will sing again!*
Confidence is violence; Julie Andrews will not sing again.

It's 1965 – the hills are alive! So are my parents. One is ten,
the other twenty-five. Martin Buber has just died – no *I & Thou* again.

Once upon a time, Pteranodons – boom! (Let's not dwell on
mass extinction. Leave it at – they will not roam again.)

Don't laugh! How did this happen? I'm mean time's abstract
and many violations: e.g., *You can't go home again.*

I will not walk into the Dublin Airport Premier Inn to find you
by the bar again; you will not drink white wine again.

I am laughing/weeping at the sound melt makes – the vacant
volubility of collapse; glaciers will cease to creep again.

The earth fractures into shards again. There is no *begin again* –
words reduce to stupid noises; how can I sing again?

The throat decays; the larynx burns to nothing.
My father liked to say, *The rest… is silence.*

Aubade

I have often rolled my eyes
at all the solo young folk
soaked through with heartache
like people waking up
some warm June dawn
beside a river or a lake,
completely wet with dew.
I've made good choices
in my life, practical choices.
I have not pinned my hopes
to an eternity of peach light
before one last descent
into a subway station or
a basement bar. I do not ramble
through the crappy parts of town,
the vast and liminal halls
of public transport, thirty-dollar
motel rooms, or Jan's diner at midnight,
contemplating, bittersweetly,
you –
I still have no idea
what I would trade
to lick your neck once more
while the thunder churns incessantly
beyond the antique, leaded window
and our magical stopwatch
working on time itself
is forever paused.

Desiderata

Bad weather, petrichor, oak pollen,
allergies, not having cancer, favourable
biopsy results: things that salt
the passage of time.

The hero's journey. Struggles
that end happily or neutrally.
Nothing gained, but nothing lost.
Severed thumbs stitched back together.

Dissolvable stitches!
Kayaks that capsize in warm water.
I want everything like a kayak
to turn upright with muscle.

Shadow folk appearing bedside
with compassion. UFO footage
released with mystery intact.
Cyclones without peril.

Marriages where no one
dreams of endings,
the feeling of endings
that never arrive,

like train delays
at peak time
if you've got wine in a can
and no responsibilities.

The Wedding at Cane Creek Farm

The sun snuck off in the middle of dinner like a hot narcissist who would not be missed.

A new moon sky in Saxapahaw is deep and long – it is the world's most endless sky!

The bride and groom were my friends. I loved them; their beauty was endless as this sky.

I had never seen two people smash glass as gleefully as they did, as tearfully, as swiftly.

Gradually the marquee emptied itself of all but the remains of the most delicious cake.

The barman recognised me; I recognised the October smell of fields cooling.

Around me, my private disappointments flopped in disarray. I struggled to tuck them in.

The broomsedge and meadow fescue formed a barrier at the edge of our clearing.

This wall of wild grasses was lit up by the bonfire.

I talked with two or three other people for whom things had also not worked out.

At the end of the night we danced near the fire like people who once loved dancing.

Every Little Helps

I have never felt so comforted
as I have at the grocery store.

I have been soothed by creme-filled cakes,
by the gaze of gherkins in their jars.

Bad feelings – I have left out in the car
to overheat and die

in the gorgeous
July weather;

among weather-less aisles
I wander in serenity and ease.

For I have seen plenty everywhere
I could not see evidence of evil:

in the relaxing sound of the ground lamb
in its bed of cold plastic,

in these perfect mounds
of Red Delicious apples.

They are not delicious.
They are really, really, really, really red.

Carol

The brass band outside Waitrose
      on the way home
is as senseless as a weapon,
      all space, all breath
      – a weapon –
is a crowd and a crowd without violence
      is not at peace and it is nothing
like the heart's panic behind the till,
behind a queue not not never-ending.

In the shop there is no day not at war,
      there is no moment
that the in-store music playlist does not sound
      like gravity, like fluorescence and the time-clock
      wounding all the parts that already hurt,
like the train home does not sound
      like I am not weeping
      into my festive sandwich –
I want to hear no people,
      only the noise of distant lights.

Night, Lamp, Street, Pharmacy

(A translation – after Alexander Blok)

Night, a street, a streetlight, a Superdrug,
an iPhone's faint and stupid light.
Even if you live for another big old chunk
of years, it's always the same. There's no way out.

You'll die – the whole dang thing restarts
from antiquity onwards, unceasingly rehashed –
darkness, bitter ripples on the river,
a Superdrug, a street, a light.

Princess Cottongrass

You have come to the end
    of almost everything
        except the tarn
    its upside-down lens
        and hearts sunk in thick varve.
In waters black, reflective
    as a locked phone screen
you see your self
    peeling away
        in long strips
           of gaze
to foolproof fugue state.
And now with only the body left –
    its warmth –
        meet theft by physics,
rubbing your nose in it,
    that time before all this
        when you believed
           in your beginning.

Goat Willow

I don't know what this fluff is called,
gathered path-side and all around,
these white, these hairy airborne –
piling up, rising past the rutted track
the tyre stack and rusted wire. I doubt
everything: that this is lovely,
that we are having a nice time,
that this wood is not a ruin,
cratered by tree fall,
all jagged deadwood –
to what end?
Have I ever lived
face-deep in catkins,
taking names?

Castle Meadows

From the top of the motte
I dream of bringing you here
to dream of history with me,

how we'll talk about the few
remaining walls, the dogs on walks
and their people dressed as if

these paths are difficult.
Though they are, I suppose,
in some ways.

Look up! I'll say, *The gates
were here – the sky has simply
plugged the murder holes.*

And we'll wonder – were
the townsfolk self-important,
the way we are.

And you will ask, *Where
did they bury everyone when
one-third of the place died?*

I'll say, *There were a bunch
more churchyards then.
Eight or nine, I read somewhere.*

You can only
imagine what you
can imagine –

there is only the self
that can be known
and that, rarely.

I'll want to tell you
not to worry.
But I am worried.

Follow the Gleam

'Aye Sir Galahad, that we might see the grail!'

The girls at summer camp are lining up
along the lakeshore, beneath the granite dome,
exiting drab cabins in their Sunday whites,

in their bold heraldic tunics,
bearing wooden swords and shields
for the last day's pageant.

They are King Arthur, Galahad.
They are the one-hundred and fifty knights
who set out and failed.

Sun-drunk, interchangeable as
ballads, they advance with
high-pitched song in single file.

Autumn, Winter follow, mulching
their hymns. Only Sir Bors, returning
to home's wilderness, will sustain a girlish faith:

that she may march towards some truth,
no one can view, that means as much
as lakes and mountains.

That Month We Walked

That month we walked around the block each night
at seven. We did not wonder too much
about the reason we were not at home.
Tent moths had spawned in all the hickories,
their limbs encased in silk as if by fog.
We stared at all the houses that were not
ours, their porch lights pulled a swarm to each front
door. The quiet smoke-grey pavement still was
warm underfoot. Mom took no pleasure in it.
She tried to grow tomatoes in the shade.
Her jeans drew fallen caterpillars. They
crept up her legs in dozens. She left them.
I heard that on their honeymoon, my father never
left the room. When, if ever, did she know?

Nymphette

At your mom's flat, in the master bath, you cut your arms
a dozen or more times, with a Bic, before the pizza came.

Me looking at you, a minor goddess! Your peach foundation (freckles
showing through) and Black Cherry lips. You fed me cheeseburgers,

chicken nuggets, ranch, barbecue, and chips after weed smoked
out of a Coke can – a shotgun full of smoke is how lungs kiss –

and it felt so good. With you. Always pleasure, all pleasures
to be known and shared between us in our black mesh dresses,

in our fishnet tights and tall boots at Frank's late night coffee shop
that did not card for mint chocolate cigarettes in a pretty tin.

Out 'til 2am, you loud – you lustrous – we made havoc all the way
to the toilets in the nice hotel. This was when you introduced

your secret stash of strawberry lollipops. In wall-sized mirrors
we watched ourselves, sucking on sweets, famished.

Pastoral Care

You were the prom dress with no body in it,
thumbing the air at the county line,
near the banks of the wide red river.
No field was looking out
for you, no shepherd stepped
from the labyrinth of the corn –
not the monstrous American
robin, its freakish stride upon
the leaf mould, nor the cows;
on the nights their calves are taken,
they think only of themselves.
No home for you – roads only.
Life is a golden pickup truck, you said,
as golden as a hay bale, heated up
in the deep core, liable to combust –
oh honey! You were the love-song
hitched to the tree frogs' chatter,
consort of the unpaved trailer park –
joyriding the fog beyond the chicken yard,
you were the mist that sighs
upon the windshield glass,
the midnight voice, crackling
with lust, the cosmic pulse
amidst the radio static –
when even the power lines
had turned their backs.

Thinking About the Chicken Bridge Murder While Riding in a Truck

Driving on a rootless road,
sitting in a wordless space,
smoke curling in his beard,
yellowing the truck's cab,
in the gunless peace
of the January cold.

She was never dressed for cold,
said her feet ached like the road,
believed she'd made her peace
with the lack of space.
There were three inside the cab
if you didn't count his beard.

The third couldn't grow a beard
and didn't mind the cold
trapped within the cab
on an empty bright black road;
it was created by this space
to learn the poverty of peace.

The diner's lights are peace
and salvation is a beard
that can pass freely through this space,
though it does nothing for the cold.
There are ten churches on this road
if you exclude the truck's cab.

A service in this cab
is as true as hunter's peace
in the woods beside the road,
but prayer gets stuck inside his beard!
He says, *It's dirty as the cold*
that coils into empty space.

Babe, belonging to this space –
sins enclosed within a cab
and arrested by the cold –
can become a kind of peace
if you embrace the steadfast beard
and erase a long dark road.

The long dark godlessness of space, the ineffectiveness of peace,
the fire in the cab, the devil curling in a beard:
Honey, what's gone is just the cold beatin' at the road.

God's Smoking Lounge

Stuck in the fug of it, this is his
everywhere, the terrible smell
of spent tobacco,

his mouth becomes
all of the air, or
prayer of the reflux cough,

passing the matchbox,
too warm beside the radiator,
the infernal coffee maker,

stubbing eternal
hand-rolled cigarettes
on every effort,

in a whoosh
exhaling Genesis,
lighting up.

Ache mushrooms,
rolls down the walls,
amid the fumes

inviting us to sit a spell,
stonewalling utterly
on his orange plaid sofa.

Grendel Mama

If my child is a monster, it is because
I am a monster. Hell is a soft play
themed sex dungeon; you spend eternity
fucking other people's dads. Eternity
is carrying a ball pit across the ocean.
And back again. And again. The balls
are made of dicks. This is where we live!
Somehow no mother ever fears
she'll be raped by her own son;
perhaps she should? A child is a monster
made of breasts; milk makes meat eaters.
All men are monsters – unpack
monster – I want to destroy this –
all I do is make excuses.

Bear Hunter's Ballad

Forget what you have eaten.
Feel not even the urge
to urinate. Dissolve. One
has never the need

to kill a man in peacetime.
The bears have walked
downriver looking as manlike
as allowed.

Stalk the path in the gaps
of the birdsong.
Become the wood's awareness.
Shoot as many as you can.

Hemdean Valley/Anthem

Here is the song of the sheep,
eating green tops of root crops,
the ghost lamb song,
song of the long ago farmer.

Here is the song of the March wind,
song of toasty colts in jackets,
and the song of the black dog

off the lead
in Hi-Vis pyjamas,
and the runner, taking him home – *Today!*

Will be so wonderful!
(Sings the runner.)
We have so many plans!
We will MAKE the day!

Here is the song of low aircraft,
its drone like the fat bluebottle
drifting over the hedgerows'
song of the muntjac's tusk –

the whole land opening
throats to holler:

What will be
will one day be
what's gone.

Street Party

We know everything the landlord doesn't know
about the neighbour's yellow roses purging bloom,
about these rows of terraces extruding
residents and sausage rolls and hand-made
bunting for a war no one remembers.
We know the part-time father talking to us
about weekends with his daughter,
and the glam blonde grandma
strutting with her ancient pug
in its two-wheeled wheelchair.
We know who's growing pot up in their loft.
We know how the white cat lost its ears.
We know who crashed through the roof
of their conservatory and
where the children go who disappear
down alleys. (They're having secret meetings.)
We know who lived in the house
we live in now and where they've gone
or haven't gone. We know Linda
across the street and two doors down,
her nights out in her bathrobe on the pavement,
howling to the cops, *I LOVED that man!*
That man who hit her lots of times.
We know this lovely heatwave
will be again and worse.
We know the river
one day will make its banks up here,
will flood Linda's house. The mould
will paint her walls –
it won't hang bunting.

The Gearagh

    I.

After the deluge,
the wooded river's
gutting, the people here

gone elsewhere sixty years
and all that's left
is water –

broad alluvial plain,
medieval ash stumps,
remains of oak, of yew

stopping the wind,
wind prodding water
before the flood retracts,

suctioning holes
big enough
for horses even

to be lost
like a man's boot
or a glacial forest.

II.

Two grey horses
terribly judgmental
step out of alders,

mud up to the hocks,
eyeing bulbously
with old looks

the chill light, at the end
of the Port Road, asking
as much as possible:

What have YOU
lately drowned
for power?

I don't know, grey horses.
I don't know a lot.
The answer is a lot.

III.

Meascán mearaí
means
bewilderment

in a language
not your own, though
you have felt it –

the ghost of
a diasporic pang.
This land will do that to you.

Slowly, from the east
the oaks grow back,
returning to confuse us.

The Twelve Swans

A dozen swans in the fog, in the anticyclonic
gloom, and the fog's grey gauze veils
their pale necks above traffic,

the way some stories
obscure the work we've done
for brothers,

while others affirm
our labours, the years spent
knitting tunics from bog cotton

only to see them cast
over bird-shapes that become men –
every single grievance numbered.

The Elvers

'Young eels have a wholesome idea that nothing can stop them;
consequently nothing does.'
— Gertrude Elizabeth Blood Campbell

'Every eel matters.'
— Glass Eels UK

Nothing matters, said the elvers
en masse, synchronously clumped
below the weir. A bit stuck.

And if nothing matters,
nothing matters, said the elvers.
Children, hush.

But most of us get EATEN!
The elvers squealed, see-thru
babies, cooked till opaque.

(Not one could recall
their larval diet of marine snow
falling through a sea within a sea.)

When you get big enough
you will be compelled
to escape the estuary

swim beyond the gyre, spawn,
disappear. Become the matter
falling through the water.

No one will ever cut you slack
like your parents did.

Elegy

Late in the year I ran out of condolences,
the supermarket shelves of my linguistic
abilities having been raided by
        all of the deaths.

This was also the season I lost the capacity
to be serious about all of the deaths;
I would discuss the deaths as lightly
        as the rotten weather.

Never mind that both made me feel cold
all the way down, such that I needed to lie
on the couch through the dark hours clutching
        a hot water bottle.

A bee can only suck one flower at a time;
so it was with me and all of the deaths.
The hot water bottle was unable to address
        all aspects of the cold.

When I wasn't engaged in the pursuit
of warmth, I was getting angry at poetry;
poetry was letting me down, failing to deliver
        its promised consolations.

Grief, it occurred to me then, had nothing
to do with poetry; rather, it took the form
of countless counterfactuals
        in my brain's rotten weather,

like if I could get on a plane and fly to Texas,
perhaps I could find you,
eating kolaches at Hruska's
        all on your lonesome.

Or if I could get in a boat and sail to Sligo
perhaps I could find you near your aunt's house,
talking about Ben Bulben like
        you had a stake in it –

When I wasn't taking on faith the gruesome
notion that the deaths had actually occurred
and arguing with myself about it, I put
        impossibility in the crosshairs –

and set myself the task of writing a poem
about all of the deaths as if such a person
as me could accomplish this feat;
        the cockeyed arrogance!

For one thing, I don't like to talk about myself
but here I am doing it again. And yet –
there didn't seem to be another way;
        we all hate a hypocrite.

For another thing, my father had died,
and I hated my father, the way people
who hate their fathers usually do;
        I don't wish to bore you.

For another thing, grief came to me at the park
or in the car on Saturday morning,
or at the kitchen sink, scraping out the porridge pot,
        leaving it to soak.

Grief was like the rusted bench frame
I passed on my daily runs, overtaken
by blackthorn. There was no sense in
        trying to sit there.

Grief was like trying to walk downhill
in mud in January and stay upright;
you need special shoes
        or something.

Grief was like the rats that ate each other
in the back alley. I couldn't speak to it;
I could only freak out on Church Street
        openly at midday.

It was about this time that every single utterance
started to sound like a song by Taylor Swift,
whom I doubted had ever suffered and
        should have kept quiet.

But me! I had suffered. I had wrapped
my grief in damp paper towel and stuck it
in a plastic bag, having got the idea from
        Gardeners' Question Time.

I looked for signs of growth,
but it only mouldered leaving
a dark-green residue on my fingers
        when touched.

I went back to poetry, growing ever-angrier
at the deceitful pause at the end
of each line, that tells us:
        this is serious.

How can it be serious? If I can say all this,
but never the words that would bring them back?
And me, like a silly, sad child who believes
        in necromancy,

who puts her hands out, wishing, talking
nonsense – loaded with the optimism
encoded in the undertaking
   of pointless undertakings.

Lemure

Some May midnight you will stand
in the red light of the dishwasher's clock,

the smell of rotten lamb's blood
rising from the U-bend.

You are considering the shapelessness
of what survives, how

every home
is haunted.

And looking away to avoid the grey-white
mask come out of the humus,

the tobacco-stained rictus of its ill-intent,
of its invincible grievances,

its hair made out of the smell
of last year's kippers –

you will get the giggles
of the petrified.

You must turn back towards
the apparently real!

Protein powder, kettle limescale.
The unwashed dishes.

The Rail Replacement Bus at Surbiton

The displaced voices of the feral parakeets
have called me here to mimic human speech.

Having chosen to sharpen the noodle
of the self, I sense there is no point to it.

The sun emits its weak September light – so mild,
so girlish it might yet turn you down.

It can access every college lawn, every private garden,
untroubled by insomnia, artless –

Not me. I have merely curdled
in the company of better folks.

I have nursed the flyblown outlook
of the hard done by.

Obsessed with infelicitous substitutions,
like myself, I have failed at the work

of garroting the ego
to face the happening of things.

I cannot
wish you

every
happiness;

I wish you
wild green birds.

The Museum of Bad Art

In my many salvaged portraits of dead pets
the essence was the fur; we loved it dearly.
And if a dog picks up a palette knife,
who is to say I am not the dog?
I have never in my life seen things as they were;
few do. Who is to say I have failed at representation?
If have neglected perspective,
it was warped from the outset.
If I left hands off the people,
it spoke to a lack of hands.
Viridian is grass enough –
there is no need to mix it.
The brushstroke's upward flick
exists already as trees.

A Compendium of Losers

Good people, trust. The aftermath of pirates.
The one who lost "the one that got away."
Doorless doorframes, Adam and Eve,
the Virgin Mary.
Off-gassing furniture
and most of Sappho's work.
Also, taxidermy, energy vampires.
Beef jerky.
King Arthur, dreaming ahead of time
how hard it sucks to fail –
we've all been there –
taking over the world,
neglecting the marital bed.
Involuntary celibates.
All those who will today
receive a boilerplate rejection note.
Ceremonial magic – it was nothing of the sort,
but poor Eliphas Levi!
And Poor Jud from *Oklahoma*.
Poor Jimi Heselden, former CEO of Segway.
Poor Rimbaud, for getting shot
and getting cancer
and making us feel sad.
Ubi sunt, the sun, the light
from long-dead stars.
Things that shed – viruses,
geckos, house cats.
The colour pink.
Trees in autumn and in drought.
Substance, sub-atomic particles,
and coal mines.
A pumpkin vine in late October.
Salmon spawning, eaten up by bears.

Every kind of bear. Ice cold rivers. Ice.
All the mothers of small children
who have not washed their hair today.
George Washington's cherry tree
myth. Christmas Hampers,
bursting with stale crackers,
broken promises of good cheer,
and excelsior. The word *hamper*,
its incompatible definitions.
The murderer we met that night near White Cross –
his lovely manners.
Six of the seven wonders.
The long-list, all but one.
Dry bones.

Run for Your Life!

I don't know what rest is –
I metabolise an infinite

surface wisdom with
a long-form coffee;

my heart is strong,
I will make it live forever

exactly like
all the other joggers

in a soup of
sweat skimmed

from rain,
thinking:

how heat can
even turn to sludge

a body, wherever
the path

thickens to shade,
fathomless

realities intrude,
their tread-caught

leavings drag –

up the hill
with a gasp,

thinking:

all things
must improve

at a gentle pace,
even a lot of nothing

evolves to tracks.

Nabokov's Genitalia Cabinet

Love, will you not hold still
just long enough
for me to pay attention?

To swoop my soft
but brutal net; to snare
but leave no damage –

I would stick you
in a fragrant old cigar box,
to taxonomize at leisure,

enraptured by the silences
you make beneath
my handy microscope –

each eye mapped and mine
the only gaze.

Mercury in Retrograde

Got to the end of some beleaguered years
hoping to skirt the grim interior of more bad time,
found myself on my back, pinned to my yoga mat,
grounded with the fear of flux, the breakage
of all things with moving parts.
A long time, I lay still, thinking it over: how
Libra balances the void. How the moon moves
west to east, despite appearances. How can
an apparently backwards motion ever be
progress in disguise? Enter Mother Earth
swinging a colostomy bag full of gemstones,
inviting me to brace myself against her guts,
offering nothing in the way of basic courage,
only this:

Expecting disappointment,
you see it everywhere.

No One Comes from No One

On days when no words
will have left your mouth,
Death need not knock –

the hours staining
magnolia walls
with increasing dark –

the pang at dusk that brings
the grackles to the pear trees
in the car park –

the phone you hold
like a pillow above
Time's cot.

The Pioneers

"Who wants a body now?" the smug ghost said
when we all got the shits from bad water.
Pulsing above the fire every night
he followed us and never let up heckling
the encampment. We felt his death never
as a lack, but more room in the wagon.
The wagon and the journey were the answer:
to die in loneliness in grasses or in snow
like bison wouldn't be the worst thing.
Think what goodness we have known in life:
to have seen lightning forking in the sky
and loved despite the presence of the ghost,
to have glimpsed beyond the fire's embers
a vacancy awaiting on dark plains.

The Extrovert

I am not a cat lady;
cats are people.
I am a people person.

At the Café des Artistes, 2006

Eighteen months to live – you must
have known it and of course you did.
Hence the Met all day, to see
the Christ with bloodshot eyes,
and the Virgin's outward facing
nausea, in search of gold,
of lapis and the salmon pink
of the Angel's pleated dress.
Now dark and frost are tightening
around 1 West 67th Street,
and the wood nymphs,
stained by sixty years'
tobacco, have outlasted
health and youth as usual.
Whatever agonies speak
deep in the marrow, do not
on the surface of this evening.
You have perfected deceit,
the art of looking away
into –
ochre light through Kir Royale,
darkening rosily at the flute's base,
and the scallops –
never again such perfect scallops!

Tuesday in Bracknell

The thin lady at the toddler group
with red marks on her cheeks and neck
looks like she is sleeping poorly
though she does not moan about it.

She is sitting on the floor among the Duplo,
cross-legged in purple lycra.
Leaning towards her child, she says,
"This is *real* magic."

I don't know what she means by that.
Her voice is low, earnest, and very sad.
She asks about my *Totoro* tote bag.
I don't ask about the marks on her face.

Later, I pass her near the park – her posture bent
as if the afternoon were a planet of its own,
bearing down its weight upon
her head, the pushchair. The changing bag.

This time I say nothing out of shame –
what could I say or offer – coffee, tea,
an hour's small talk, an intention
to meet again, a number for support?

Then off she goes on foot. I stay behind
to dissect my guilt. *Please*, I want to say,
go get your proof of Otherworlds.
Please find real magic.

Eating a Danish Alone on a Friday

There is a pastry I always get
at the Ole and Steen by the bus stop

and when I eat it, it tastes almost exactly
like the ones I had when I was young.

This coffee is not very good
and that too is like the past,

but the cup is compostable –
it is not like the past at all.

At the old bakery – I was probably eight –
there was a poster of Neuschwanstein

and model wedding cakes and I hoped
for a future full of these cakes and alpine vacations…

I'm not sure if it's enough – these lulls
when the world is briefly custard.

Cholsey Station: Staring Down the Well of the Present Moment

I have had some issues lately
with the sunlight hanging
from the bodies of the villagers
for years
along the concrete platform –

I have made complaints
about the winter barley
on the smooth, adjacent hillside
its mild eruptions
disrupting the horizon –

Tell me, is there time
to run back to
the coffee lady
with her tiny car
and purple hair?

Double Rainbow

Good, but not for long – that lime green line
at the sky's heart splits two bands of colour where
a washed-out violet hovers highest. There is nothing
better than a sign that means nothing, no luck but this
moment digging into the lack of pain, the sufficiency
of certain circumstances. Free now from malice
for a time, family graves lie elsewhere –
the earth smell after rain especially becomes them,
the darkening sycamores and cedar. If one could behold
this space in every aspect – grey slate roofs a lighter tint
than storm, than wires, than the fat grey long-haired cat
in next door's garden? It's fair to say the light
and tiny droplets ever present in the stuff of day
could make this any time. We know when to look for it.
I love you breathing, alive, and not too cold.

Sourwood

It is embarrassing –
that I expected to see you.
though our cars are parked
a quarter-century apart
and each is fastened
to its moment.
The view from here,
as far as I remember,
was blue trees for miles;
a trick of isoprene,
of atmosphere, of light.
Memory is story;
story is a choice.
You were never one
to make an effort.
I don't know why
I thought I could,
not cross paths exactly,
but close some distances?
Nope.
Instead of you,
I meet only what
I had forgotten –
how mica sheds its glitter
down the paths,
how it fractures; tiny bits
spangle the riverbed.
The streams, the falls –
I had forgotten these.
Feral water,
slow-motion
melt of gneiss.

I want to tell you
that I never lied, and
I have realised this
was not a kindness.
I may have some learnings yet.
The honeybee is at the sourwood,
beside the white bells of its bloom,
dancing to no music.

Notes on the Eleusinian Mysteries

Every season is a wilderness. Like a lot of us, Demeter was a good girl.
High achieving. Putting her body into it, dead serious about growth.

She has the kind of job that gives you IBS – it's *that* relentless.
But Kore is inertia's darling: a seed eater. Nothing sprouts inside a gut.

November – there's a medlar tree at my work. I think about the pomegranate and also rot as food. Bletting isn't rot, just softening. Time pulps me too.

Trying to convince myself that death is only half of things, trying not to see it, I hurt so much. I am so lonely. I can't remember laughing with friends.

Enter the Lord of the Many; he appears before me at Ikea. We eat meatballs beneath huge air ducts; I am willing this to be Thanksgiving dinner.

Not even the olives with their splendid fruit could hear her screams.
Try screaming with a mouth full of olives. Meatballs. Seeds.

*

Demeter – did she ever wonder if she'd have had the trouble she had,
if she had been somebody else? She has time to kill each winter;

perhaps she lifts weights to be strong and thin. But not too thin.
To be just right. Meanwhile her daughter –

any child of an ambitious mother will know the relief occasioned by
escape, even taken by her uncle/lover: here is a chance to become more

truly yourself, Lady of the Many. Mother-cravings – dormant. You can
unite the worlds above and below; you don't even need a mom for this.

And mom? Anguished above ground, feeling so hard the insult of warmth
– what would happen if she stopped gouging herself on want?

Nah, she's on the move. She's on the hunt for Kore, finding it painful
to witness human families, the size of them, massive and loud –

the malignant uncles, the judgmental aunts – they rarely steal
one another's children. There is hardly any incest at all.

*My friend Jackie says human interaction is haunted by past selves,
past conversations, the lives we had before. Is this a human interaction?*

*I try to understand you, your terrible outbursts,
the fear of family, the fear of love, the fear of home –*

*critters like us
can't deal
with a life's freight
of loss.*

*

Seeing what's still here: that is, *what* remains, versus
"the remains" or "human remains" – this is hard.

Demeter doesn't bother. She does not write a memoir or go on a river cruise –
she throws a tantrum. The rest of us, thrashing gets us nowhere –

who can we turn into short-eared owls in our rage?
Who will take us in? The problem, I realise, is Demeter –

putting a baby into the fire – and you, not knowing a good thing
when it was putting your baby in the fire! Raise your hand

if you have never mistaken loss for lost. If you never
put your baby in the fire, you fucked up the fire.

*

*January – I make vague plans to watch torches being carried
through an orchard; the fire is handheld. There is a crowd.*

*The crowd suggests the membrane of night can be
punctured or burst, as long as we are doing it together.*

*Outside it is not dawn, the plums at the allotments are okay
as trees in the dark, with leaves or without leaves,*

*half-buried, needing no one, not even the suggestion
that what's underground ought to come above.*

*

Back in the meadow, the maidens tend to their maidenly pastimes,
like buttercup identification – there are two-thousand species.

They twine green stems around their fingers. Their bodies indent
a plush bed of sweet vernal-grass. No one has hay fever, the earth

already in bloom, anticipates return. *The practice of rebirth:
dress rehearsal for a show that never opens?*

In the Mysteries, the earth opens itself with help
from no one. *Cue a joke about some lady's privates –*

this is the most important part of the event – when Demeter laughs
at Baubo, at her vulva, at the hilarious boy popping out between her legs –

essential because she needed missing punctured.
Lift up your skirts, dear world! Lift up your skirts.

Happy New Year!

If we have not cried even a little bit tonight,
if our laughter poked at life as if it were
the skin grown on cooled milk,
pulled it clean off –
Whatever power denial holds
for the lighthearted,
we seize like canapés –
This is the year we will go
full Orpheus, the year
we finally become someone
other than ourselves.
We will learn a language
without trying, eat without
trying, pray without trying.
 The minutes gutter to the countdown's pit,
resolve into a blonde drink's fizz,
an emptied clock-shaped saucer.

To Edward D Wood Jr—An Invocation

'This is a pathetic buffoon... Pretty, but ineffectual and tragic'
— Maila Nurmi

Bring on the beefcakes in the leopard skirts,
I am making this thing happen, 100%,
I am serious about the occult,
pornography and getting drunk, the ritual
of making it – the sex-filled graveyard.
My soul is 100% juddering
down Sepulveda Boulevard, yoked
to a dream of ghouls, courageous
with its wagon of fog and the soundstage.
I am eating a diet of 100% smut
and cheesecake – I am a total genius!
My enthusiasm for 100%
black polyester capes is 110%!
I am an ecstasy of bronze prop skulls
and the exploitation of my dreams.
I am the fancy psychic, I am the
hot uncanny lady dressed in black.
My heart is 100% pitching
at all times, 100% I am getting
the funds together, 150%
in debt, evicted from
the antique casket,
me and my alter-ego
in her numinous cosy sweater
and I am awe-struck
by the angora's marvellous
backlit nimbus on set.

The Opposite of Ocean

The many blues
the landscape owns –
I want them all.

I want cold melon soda.
I want to be a bride.
To drive cross-country

with men. Make a scrapbook.
I want the fritto misto at
the Gower Seafood Hut.

Attachment, I inhabit
cattywampus, leaking
brain-wise, a dissociative

transatlantic shock;
I hold to nothing, deracinated,
plonked, happily sinking

in the estuarine sediment.
    Land-sick, the beach
sways from the knees up;

get me a windowless
interior room, the sewage
smell of ship's water.

I want actual
dolphins. White horses
made of waves.

I spend entire workdays
whistling
into the storm.

Enta Geweorc

Get in the ancient hot tub, sexy friend!
Get in the old hot water. Loll with me –
there will come a time when
there is no one left to do this work –
get in the hot tub now while we still
have hot water; the human heart
overwhelmed and fitful, need not engage
the double disappearance of the past
and the past's past – we will go for tapas
after! We will drink an Albariño
that tastes like green apples,
we will throw the moonlight over
our shoulders like salt.

The Pleasure Club

Stumbling towards the daytime party, the summer humid and loud
in the pine wood, the quarry lake filled in with the reflection of trees
– here is a cold beer bottle. Press it against your sunburned face.
You have agreed to the spiritual practice of brunch. You have agreed
to encase your thighs in cut-off denim. You have taken erotic literature
into your heart. You have taken a flatpack Pleasure Dome
into the insensitive world; this is your lodestar: visit every nude spa,
eat French fries with no underpants. Take a stand for games.
You will climb mountains to the bar at the summit. If there is no bar,
you will find a better mountain. You will pootle on your bike.
You will leap and long. You will gallop like a feral dog.
You will hold your lover's face between your hands
like a giant hotdog. But first: here is the trail leading back
to the party; you will trip over your feet until you reach
a potluck dinner in a cottage with friends. The lamps are off,
except a year-round string of Christmas lights. There will be
a balm in this house, the pursuit of survival. The world still exists
for another day and another – please believe, for once, you can be
loved. The screen door's constant clap announces welcome.

Two Rivers Press has been publishing in and about Reading
since 1994. Founded by the artist Peter Hay (1951–2003),
the press continues to delight readers, local and further afield,
with its varied list of individually designed,
thought-provoking books.